MY WHOLE 30 DIET RECIPES

Delicious, Healthy and easy-to-cook recipes for your nutritional reset: A plan to help change your life forever.

By

TOM WESTWOOD

Copyright © 2019 by: TOM WESTWOOD

ISBN-13: 978-1-950772-46-9

ISBN-10: 1-950772-46-2

All Rights Reserved. No part of this publication may be reproduced in any form or by any means, including scanning, photocopying, or otherwise without prior written permission of the copyright holder.

Disclaimer:

The information provided in this book is designed to provide helpful information on the subjects discussed. The publisher and author are not responsible for any specific health or allergy needs that may require medical supervision and are not liable for any damages or negative consequences from any treatment, action, application or preparation, to any person reading or following the information in this book.

Table of Contents

INTRODUCTION 6

    IT START WITH FOOD 6

THE WHOLE 30 DAY RECIPES TO TOTAL HEALTH AND FOOD FREEDOM 8

    Salmon Salad (an Alternative to Tuna) 8

    Shrimp Spread with Dill 9

    Simplified Grilled Eggplant Involtini 11

    Snow Pudding (Sugar-Free) 13

    Sugar-Free Custard Sauce (Stirred Custard, Soft Custard 15

    Coconut Cake (Low-Carb Sugar-Free) 16

    Mexican Grilled Chicken Marinade 18

    New World Pumpkin Soup 19

    North Carolina BBQ Chicken Sauce 21

    Old-Fashioned Low-Carb Meat Loaf 22

    Oven-Baked Rutabaga "Fries" 24

    Oven-Baked Salmon with Herbs 25

    Pecan Nut Pie Crust 26

    Low-Carb Pumpkin Pecan Pancakes 27

    Seared Scallops 29

    Quick Chicken Alfredo with Shirataki Noodles 30

    Lemon Cheesecake 32

    Roasted Brussels Sprouts 35

    Skillet Chicken Divan 36

    St. Louis Barbecue Sauce 38

    Stir-Fried Kung Pao Chicken with Chili Peppers 39

    Strawberry Chicken Salad 41

    Strawberry Vinaigrette 43

Almond Spice Cookies 44

Easy Baby Back Ribs 46

Cranberry Walnut Cookies 48

Sugar-Free Chocolate Pecan Torte 50

Peanut Butter Cups (Low Carb) 52

Fresh Berry Pie(Sugar-Free) 54

Super-Easy Guacamole 56

Piquant Sauce for Meatloaf (Low Carb) 57

Chengdu Chicken 58

Terri's Tofu Scramble 60

Tuna Walnut Salad 62

Tzatziki with Mint - Cucumber Yogurt Sauce or Side Dish 63

Vegan Curried Tofu and Walnut Salad Recipe 64

Sugar-Free Instant Pumpkin Pudding 65

Warm Spinach Salad with Hot Bacon Dressing 67

Watermelon Salad with Cucumber and Mint 69

Blueberry Cream Cheese Coffeecakes 70

"Doughnut" Muffins 73

Gnocchi 75

Biscotti 78

Zucchini "Pasta" 81

Crust less Smoked Salmon, Leek, and Mushroom Quiche 83

Zesty Grilled Shrimp 85

Unstuffed Cabbage 87

Thousand Island Dressing 89

Warm Spinach Salad with Hot Bacon Dressing 90

Watermelon Salad with Cucumber and Mint 92

Cream Cheese Frosting 93

Banana Bread 94

Coconut Shrimp 96
CONCLUSION 98

INTRODUCTION
IT START WITH FOOD

To lose weight is not a shake, a supplement, or an exercise gizmo. The major key to your weight-loss success! Is right there at your fingertips. I feel the major action you can take when battling to lose weight is to keep a food diary. It is time sapping to write down everything consumed during the day, but this in itself can curtail overeating and be vital for self-assessment and monitoring. Studies shows that more than 3,000 people who have lost an average of 66 pounds and kept it off forever–found that keeping a food journal is the major strategy used by the majority of successful dieters

However, if you keep track on the food you consume, it will force you to take responsibility for your food choices. Keeping an accurate food journal and monitoring the foods you eat helps you see eating patterns, giving you an insight into when and why you eat and above all estimate calorie intake, so we can make adjustments, by eating less or exercising more.

Nevertheless, if your rate of weight loss has slowed down rapidly despite your sticking to your plan, take a sincere look at your eating and exercise routine. It will pinpoint where you are a star, and where you may be falling short in your efforts.

Sticking on a diets truly work. Moreover, every book, article, fitness plan, regimen etc. works as long as you stick to it. Getting yourself motivated is arguably the most essential part of losing weight. You should know that the information will always be there at your door step, but the motivation to stick to a diet is the thing that everyone wants and few of us have. So if I may ask how you do get motivated to stick to a diet and stay on track, and most importantly, to get where you want to go. Ask yourself right now, "Why do you really want to lose weight"? At first glance, this may sound like a self-explanatory question, but at the long run if you are struggling with your weight, you need to ask yourself this question continuously until you come up with a very clear answer.

Finally, you have to create a compelling picture of how sexy you going to look if you lose the weight or worse if you do not. Then you cultivate this picture and let it be your motivating factor in your weight loss program. When you are motivated, you will be much close to taking the necessary action needed.

MY WHOLE 30 DIET RECIPES

THE WHOLE 30 DAY RECIPES TO TOTAL HEALTH AND FOOD FREEDOM

Salmon Salad (an Alternative to Tuna)

Ingredients:

½ cup of minced onion

½ cup of mayonnaise

Fresh herbs (if you wish)

2 cans of salmon (about 16 oz. each)

2 medium stalk celery (minced, including leaves)

2/3 cup of sugar-free pickle relish

Directions:

All you do is mix all ingredients together.

Notes:

1. I prefer to use Mt. Olive Sugar-free Sweet Pickle Relish for this recipe

2. In the other hand, if you don't have sugar-free sweet relish available, I suggest you use dill relish or chopped up dill pickle -- sweeten if you wish with zero-carb sweetener.

3. However, if you have fresh herbs, I suggest you add 3 or so Tablespoons, chopped. Chives, dill, parsley, and tarragon all work perfectly.

NUTRITIONAL INFORMATION

Amount per serving: 1 serving size

Calories: 270

Fiber: ½ g

Carbohydrate: 2g

Protein: 23g

Shrimp Spread with Dill

Tips:

1. Feel free to also make this recipe with crab.

2. Remember, fresh dill is best, but dried is Okay - use 2 tablespoons or you can substitute a different herb if you don't have dill.

3. However, if you have low carb ketchup, I suggest you use it, if not use the lemon juice and sweetener. (You should know that the tomato flavor isn't as important as the combination of sweet and sour in the ketchup.)

Ingredients:

½ cup of regular mayonnaise (however, if low fat cream cheese is used, 6 Tablespoons of mayonnaise)

2 cups of fresh chopped dill (loosely packed)

6 green onions (chopped)

1 teaspoon of garlic powder

Pinches of black pepper

2 Tablespoons of lemon juice and 2 teaspoons of sugar substitute

16 oz. cream cheese (preferably regular or low fat, at room temperature)

16 oz. cooked shrimp (feel free to use fresh, frozen, or canned)

2 stalk celery (minced)

2 Tablespoons of Worcestershire sauce

A few drops of hot sauce (such as Tabasco)

½ cup of low carb catsup OR

Directions:

1. First, you chop shrimp, or pulse in food processor to a rough chop.

2. However, if you using a food processor, I suggest you remove shrimp at this point.

3. After which you put the other ingredients in a food processor and pulse until smooth.

4. Then you taste and adjust seasonings.

NUTRITIONAL INFORMATION (with regular cream cheese)

Amount per serving: 1 serving size

Calories: 1475

Fiber: 2g

Carbohydrate: 15g

Protein: 65g

NUTRITIONAL INFORMATION (low fat cream cheese)

Amount per serving: 1 serving size

Calories: 1106

Fiber: 2g

Carbohydrate: 25g

Protein: 72g

Simplified Grilled Eggplant Involtini

Ingredients:

Salt

2 cups of ricotta cheese

½ teaspoon of pepper

2 cups of sugar-free pasta sauce (from a jar)

2 large eggplants (sliced lengthwise, ¼ inch thick - aim for 16 slices)

2 tablespoons of olive oil

½ cup of shredded Parmesan cheese

Pinches of nutmeg

2 cups of mozzarella cheese

Directions:

1. First, you lightly salt the eggplant slices and let stand up to one hour. (However, if you have no much time, you can actually skip this step - I don't think it makes a huge difference.)

2. After which you mix up the Parmesan cheese, ricotta cheese, nutmeg, pepper, and chives.

3. After that, you wipe off the eggplant slices with a paper towel and smear them with the oil (as for me I usually just drizzle the oil over and smear them with my hands, but feel free to use a brush if you'd rather.)

4. At this point, you grill the eggplant, either on a grill pan or an outdoor grill.

5. Then you cook for about 2-3 minutes per side. Remember, you want a little char on them, and you want them to be flexible but not overly soft.

Direction for Assemble.

1. First, you put a heaping tablespoon of the ricotta mixture in the center of the slice, and roll or wrap lengthwise.

2. After which you repeat with the other slices.

3. At that, you put each serving (2 roll-ups) on a microwave-proof plate.

4. Then you spoon 2 tablespoons of the pasta sauce on top of each, and sprinkle with 2 tablespoons of the mozzarella cheese.

5. Finally, you heat each plate until cheese on top melts.

NUTRITIONAL INFORMATION

Amount per serving: 4 serving size

Calories: 278

Fiber: 6g

Carbohydrate: 10g

Protein: 17g

Snow Pudding (Sugar-Free)

Tips:

1. This recipe is light, delicious, and has almost no carbs, fat, or calories.

2. Feel free to serve with custard sauce or raspberry sauce.

3. Feel free to also substitute lime juice for the lemon, or use some of each.

Ingredients:

2 Cups of boiling water

6 eggs whites

2 Tablespoons of plain gelatin powder with 1/2 cup of cold water

Artificial sweetener to equal 1 cup of sugar (preferably a zero carb sweetener such as liquid sucralose is best

½ cup of lemon juice

Directions:

1. First, you mix the gelatin with the cold water in a large mixing bowl.

2. After which you let sit for about 2 minutes to soften.

3. After that, you add boiling water and stir to dissolve.

4. Then you add sweetener and lemon juice and place uncovered in refrigerator to cool.

5. At this point, you stir every 10 minutes or so, until it begins to thicken (this could take up to about 1 hour).

6. However, with mixer on high, you beat gelatin mixture for about 1 to 2 minutes until fully frothy.

7. Remember that a whisk attachment helps. Feel free to use a regular whisk, but be prepared for some arm exercise!

8. This is when you add egg whites and beat until stiff (preferably soft peaks are good enough if they hold their shape fairly well) this might be another 2 to 5 minutes, so I suggest you keep checking.

9. In addition, you leave in bowl or transfer to another bowl or mold.

10. After which you refrigerate – feel free to serve it any time, but it will set up well in about 15 minutes.

11. Finally, you serve with custard sauce, or defrost some frozen raspberries and sweeten to taste, for this makes a nice sauce.

NUTRITIONAL INFORMATION

Serving size: 8 serving size

Calories: 11

Fiber: 2g

Carbohydrate: ½ g

Sugar-Free Custard Sauce (Stirred Custard, Soft Custard

Ingredients:

1 ¼ milk and ½ cup of cream or preferably 2 cups of milk

Artificial sweetener to equal 4 tablespoons of sugar

6 egg yolks

½ teaspoons of vanilla

¼ teaspoon of salt

Directions:

1. First, you heat the milk or milk and cream until scalding, but if it's steaming, it's probably there. As for me I do it in the microwave.

2. After which you add the vanilla, sweetener, and salt to the milk.

3. After that, you beat the egg yolks and add a little of the milk and mix well (note that this is called "tempering" the eggs so they don't cook).

4. At this point, you repeat, adding a little more milk so you gradually bring the eggs up to temperature.

5. Then you put a small amount of water in the bottom of a double boiler or preferably a pot on which you can put a bowl and heat.

NOTE: make sure the water does not touch the bottom of the bowl.

1. In addition, you add milk and egg mixture and stir or whisk over hot/boiling water until mixture begins to thicken, after which you then remove from heat and stir until it coats a spoon. 2. Finally, you can refrigerate.

NUTRITIONAL INFORMATION

Serving size: 8 serving size

Calories: 60

Carbohydrate: 1.5g

Coconut Cake (Low-Carb Sugar-Free)

Ingredients:

½ teaspoon of cream of tartar

2 cups of coconut flour

1 ¼ teaspoons of salt

4 teaspoons of vanilla

2 teaspoons of baking powder

24 egg whites

16 egg yolks

1 cup of melted coconut oil or preferably butter, or (my favorite) ½ cup of each

2 cups of water

Sugar substitute equal to 2 ½ cups of sugar (preferably liquid)

2 teaspoons of coconut extract (or preferably Coconut Sugar-Free Syrup such as Da Vinci's to substitute for part of the sweetener and water).

Directions:

1. Meanwhile, heat oven to a temperature of 350 F.

2. After which you prepare 13X9 pan by greasing with butter or coconut oil.

3. At this point, separate the eggs, being careful that no yolk gets into the whites (as for me I usually separate the whites one at a time into a small dish, and then dump it into the mixing bowl to be perfectly sure I didn't mess it up).

4. However, if you get yolk or any oil into the egg whites or the bowl, they will not foam up properly, so I suggest that the bowl be totally clean.

5. In addition, beat egg whites with cream of tartar (note that this improves the stability of the beaten whites).

6. Then continue until white's form peaks when beaters are lifted (its fine if the peaks are soft).

7. On the other hand, if you are going to use the bowl, I suggest you beat the whites in as the main mixing bowl, after which you transfer the whites to another bowl for now (there is no need to clean the main bowl).

8. This is when you beat the eight yolks until smooth, and then add the salt, melted coconut oil and/or butter, coconut flour, vanilla, sweetener, water, extract, and baking powder in main mixing bowl and then mix well.

9. Furthermore, you add about a third of the egg white to the batter and mix in with a spatula (please do not mix vigorously or use beaters, as you do not want to deflate the foam too much).

10. After which you fold in half of the remaining whites, and then the final amount (Note: It is OK if there are a few streaks of white remaining).

11. After that, you pour batter into prepared pan and even off.

12. Then you bake for about 30-40 minutes, or until toothpick inserted in center comes out clean (at this point surface will be lightly browned.

13. Finally, you cool completely before cutting into 24 pieces. Note:

1. Remember, this cake should be kept in the refrigerator after cooling, as a result of the high egg content.

2. In the other hand, the coconut fiber will continue to attract water in humid weather. However, this can be partially prevented by the refrigeration, therefore after a couple of days, freezing will do a better job of preserving it.

NUTRITIONAL INFORMATION

Serving size: 12 serving size

Calories: 169

Fiber: 1g

Carbohydrate: 1g

Protein: 6g

Mexican Grilled Chicken Marinade

Ingredients

½ cup of water

½ teaspoon of hot powdered Chile such as cayenne

2 teaspoons of dried thyme

Pinches of cloves

2 teaspoons of garlic powder

1 cup of oil, olive or other

½ cup of lime juice

4 tablespoons of powdered ancho chilies (or preferably other mild chilies)

2 teaspoons of oregano

4 teaspoons of cinnamon

3 teaspoons of salt

6 tablespoons of sugar substitute

Directions:

1. First, mix lime juice and water, and then whisk all the other ingredients, ending with the oil.

2. Then marinate chicken for about 4 to 6 hours before grilling.

New World Pumpkin Soup

Ingredients

24 oz. of fresh (Mexican) chorizo, (or you can substitute other spicy sausage)

6 cloves garlic (put through a press or minced fine)

2 teaspoons of dried oregano

2/3 Cup of dry white wine

4 cups of chicken broth (or equivalent chicken flavoring such as a base)

1 cup of minced cilantro (and extra leaves for garnish)

4 cups of pumpkin puree (or two 15 oz. can of pumpkin)

2/3 cup of minced onion

2 teaspoons of mild ground chilies, such as ancho, (or preferably a small amount of a hotter chili)

2 tablespoons of olive oil

1 cup of heavy cream

1 cup of milk (or preferably unsweetened soy milk)

Directions:

1. First, put onion in saucepan with olive oil over medium-high heat.

2. However, if you using fresh chorizo, take it out of the skin and break it up into the pan.

3. After which you cook until sausage is browning.

4. After that, add garlic and stir for about 30-60 seconds until fragrant.

5. Then add some black pepper (about 1 teaspoon).

6. This is when you add wine and stir to loosen everything up.

7. At this point, add the rest of the ingredients except the cilantro, ending with the chicken broth.

8. In addition, add as much broth as you need to make it the thickness you want and also salt to taste.

9. Finally, before you serve, make sure you stir in the minced cilantro, and put a few leaves on each bowl of soup for garnish.

North Carolina BBQ Chicken Sauce

Ingredients

½ cup of ketchup (approximately 120 mL)

2 tablespoons Worcestershire sauce (approximately 30 mL)

2 teaspoons hot pepper sauce (approximately 10 mL)

1 cup apple cider vinegar (approximately 240 mL)

2 tablespoons brown sugar (approximately 30 mL)

1 tablespoon butter (approximately 15 mL)

2 teaspoons salt (approximately 10 mL)

Directions:

1. First, mix all ingredients together in a sauce pan.

2. After which you let simmer for about 10 minutes.

3. Then once the chicken is cooked, you shred and add sauce to coat.

Old-Fashioned Low-Carb Meat Loaf

Tips:

1. In this recipe I used TVP to absorb some of the juices produced by the meat as it cooks.

2. However, if you have trouble finding TVP (TSP), you can skip it.

Ingredients

2 cups of TVP

4 cloves garlic, minced (or preferably 2 teaspoons of garlic powder)

2 teaspoons of dried thyme

1 teaspoon of black pepper

4 tablespoons of Worcestershire sauce

½ cup of water (or preferably milk)

4 lbs. of ground meat (85% to 90% lean works well, for me, I've used beef, turkey, and combinations).

½ cup of finely chopped onion (or 2 tablespoons of dehydrated onion flakes)

2 teaspoons of dry mustard powder

2 teaspoons of dried sage

4 teaspoons of salt

4 teaspoons of salt

2 eggs

Directions:

1. First, mix all ingredients together in a bowl (Using your hands make it easier, but don't over mix).

2. After which you bake in a loaf pan, several small loaf pans, or make individual ones.

3. After that, bake at a temperature of 350 F for about 1 hour for a large loaf.

4. Remember that muffin-cup meatloaves cook in about 15 to 20 minutes.

5. However, to be sure the meatloaf is done, I suggest you insert a meat thermometer, which should reach 155 F in the center of the loaf.

6. When it is about 10 to 15 minutes before you think the meatloaf will be done, you can cover it with sugar-free picante sauce.

NUTRITIONAL INFORMATION

Amount per serving: each of 8 serving

Calories: 263

Fiber: 2g

Carbohydrate: 2g

Protein: 30g

Oven-Baked Rutabaga "Fries"

Ingredients

Olive Oil

Salt, garlic powder, and paprika

Rutabagas

Directions:

1. Meanwhile, heat oven to a temperature of 425 F.

2. After which you peel rutabagas with a paring knife and slice in ¼ " rounds.

3. Feel free to do them in strips, they will cook a little faster, but you have to watch them carefully or they'll burn.

4. After that, smear with oil and a little salt and put them on a nonstick baking sheet.

5. Then cook for about 12 minutes, turning twice.

6. Finally, take out when golden brown and tender and immediately sprinkle with garlic powder and paprika. I love to add kosher salt at the end.

NUTRITIONAL INFORMATION

Amount per serving: 1 cup raw sliced rutabaga

Calories: 50

Fiber: 3.5g

Carbohydrate: 7g

Oven-Baked Salmon with Herbs

Ingredients

4 - 8 Tablespoons of fresh herbs, chopped (thyme or dill is nice, but anything of your choice is probably good)

2 teaspoons of oil (if that - you just need a very thin film)

2 salmon filet (about 2 pound)

1 teaspoon of pepper

1 teaspoon of salt (i.e. a bit more if kosher, or if fish is skinned)

Directions:

a. First, heat the oven to a temperature of 200 F (not a typo).

b. After which you chop up the herb, and mix it with the salt and pepper (as for me I happen to have lemon thyme in my garden, and it is my favorite for fish, but regular thyme or preferably any herb you like works just fine, even parsley).

2. However, if you want to use more, that's okay, and sometimes I mix in a tablespoon or so of sesame seeds. After that, you smear the oil on an oven-proof serving platter, and put the fish on top.

3. At this point, if the filet is skinned, put some salt and pepper on both sides, otherwise just put the fish skin side down and season the top. As for me, I usually run my oily hand from the platter-smearing over the fish so the seasoning will stick a little better.

4. Then bake for about 40 to 45 minutes, until salmon flakes (moreover, you won't believe how good it is). As for me, I prefer serving it with a sort of homemade tartar sauce mixing mayonnaise, lemon zest and juice, some of the same herb I used on the fish, capers, and a very small amount of hot sauce.

NUTRITIONAL INFORMATION

Amount per serving: 3 serving per pound

Calories: 230

Protein: 30g

Pecan Nut Pie Crust

Tips:

1. This recipe is a great pie crust, particularly for pumpkin pie, but feel free to use it for other custard/pudding fillings.

2. It assist to start out with pecans from the freezer, because then the butter blends through but quickly sets up so the "mass" is pliable and easy to mold onto the sides of the pan.

3. It also a low-carb, gluten-free, and sugar-free recipe.

Ingredients

4 Tablespoons of melted butter

4 Tablespoons of sugar equivalent from artificial sweetener of your choice

2 cups of pecan pieces (preferably, frozen)

Directions:

1. First, take pecans out of the freezer and measure them into a food processor (feel free to use a blender, but be careful not to blend them down too small).

2. After which you pulse the processor until the largest pieces are as big as lentils or split peas.

3. After that, add the butter and the sweetener (I prefer liquid Splenda).

4. At this point, blend until it's mixed evenly.

5. Then dump it into a pie pan, and push with your fingers to cover the bottom and sides. Remember that it should be the right consistency to mold the crust evenly to the pie pan.

NUTRITIONAL INFORMATION

Amount per serving: whole crust

Calories: 950

Fat: 101g

Fiber: 10.5g

Carbohydrate: 4.5g

Protein: 10g

Low-Carb Pumpkin Pecan Pancakes

Ingredients

4 teaspoons of cinnamon

1 teaspoon of baking powder

½ cup of canned pumpkin

½ cup of sugar-free ginger ale (or preferably water and sweetener to taste)

4 eggs

2 cups of pecans

1 teaspoon of nutmeg

Pinches of salt

4 Tablespoons of oil

An Extra sweetener to taste

Directions:

1. First, grind pecans in food processor.

2. After which you add spices, salt, and baking powder and pulse until well-blended.

3. After that, transfer these dry ingredients to a medium-sized bowl or quart-sized measuring cup with lip. (**Note:** please do not try blending the wet ingredients with dry in the food processor, this is because it makes the batter thinner for some reason.)

4. At this point, combine the rest of the ingredients and mix well (a fork works fine).

5. Then heat pan or griddle to medium heat and cook pancakes, flipping when brown.

6. Finally, if you plan to serve the pancakes with sugar-free syrup, no extra sweetener is added, but if you're serving plain, I suggest you add an extra 2-4 tablespoons of sugar equivalent in a sugar substitute. I like the liquid forms of sucralose (Splenda) which has no extra carb in it.

NUTRITIONAL INFORMATION

Amount per serving: 1 serving size (1 pancake)

Calories: 186

Fiber: 2g

Carbohydrate: 2g

Protein: 4g

Seared Scallops

Ingredients

2 Tablespoons of oil (or preferably butter)

Salt and pepper

2 pounds of sea scallops

Directions:

1. First, you dry the scallops with paper towels.

2. After which you salt and pepper both sides.

3. After that, you heat a large regular (not non-stick) pan for about 2-3 minutes so it is quite hot.

4. Then you add the oil or butter, and then the scallops and make sure you don't let them touch each other.

5. However, if your pan is not big enough to do them all at once, I suggest you keep the first batch under a piece of foil and do two batches.

6. At this point, you cook the scallops about 1½ minutes each side.

7. Remember that they should have a golden crust on both ends, and the center should still look translucent after which you turn with tongs.

8. Make sure you serve immediately.

Directions on Serving Suggestions: make sure you serve with greens sautéed in garlic with a squeeze of lemon, with mushrooms in garlic and wine, as part of an elegant salad, or better still lots of other ways.

NUTRITIONAL INFORMATION

Amount per serving: 1 serving size

Calories: 132

Carbohydrate: 3.5g

Protein: 25g

MY WHOLE 30 DIET RECIPES

Quick Chicken Alfredo with Shirataki Noodles

Tips:

1. This recipe is a fast and easy meal which the whole family will (probably) cherish and if you really want to cut down on time you can buy vegetables that are already chopped and chicken and bacon that are already cooked.

2. As for me, I cook up a package of bacon at a goal, and then store it in the refrigerator rolled in paper toweling inside a plastic bag (Note that you can include whichever non-starchy vegetables you want).

Ingredients

2 Tablespoons of oil for sautéing

½ cup of chopped onion

2 small red Bell pepper (chopped)

2 (15 oz.) jar of Alfredo sauce

6 slices cooked bacon, crumbled

3 lb. of raw chicken breast (or better still 36-40 oz. cooked)

2 medium bunch broccoli, cut into florets (feel free to peel and chop stems also) - about 3lb.

16 oz. of sliced mushrooms

4 packages of shirataki noodles (8 oz. each, feel free to substitute for other low-carb pasta)

Optional small amount of hot sauce

Directions: Note:

1. However, if you are cooking the chicken, know that it will go faster if you sauté the onions, peppers, and mushrooms in a separate pan, and cook the broccoli in the microwave, but if you do not want to mess up more pans, I suggest you just do the following steps sequentially instead of at goal.

2. First, prepare broccoli and cook in microwave with a small amount of water.

3. After which you chop onion, and begin to sauté' in one pan with half the oil.

4. After that, cut up chicken breast and cook in other pan.

5. Then add mushrooms to onions and cook until beginning to shrink, then add chopped pepper.

6. At this point, rinse shirataki noodles in hot water and cut up with scissors.

7. Finally, you combine all ingredients and serve.

NUTRITIONAL INFORMATION

Amount per serving: 1 serving

Calories: 426

Fiber: 5g

Carbohydrate: 14g

Protein: 41g

Lemon Cheesecake

Ingredients

Ingredient for the Crust:

3 cups of almond meal

6 Tablespoons of sugar equivalent in artificial sweetener

4 Tablespoons of butter (melted)

Ingredients for the Filling:

2 ½ cups of sugar equivalent in artificial sweetener (preferably liquid)

½ teaspoon of salt

½ cup of lemon juice (preferably fresh)

½ cup of heavy cream

3 lbs. (6 packages) of cream cheese, room temperature

3 teaspoons of vanilla extract

8 eggs (room temperature)

2 Tablespoons of lemon zest

Ingredients for the Topping:

Juice and zest from 2 medium lemons (about 4 Tablespoons of juice and 2 Tablespoons of zest)

1 teaspoon of vanilla extract

2 cups of sour cream

½ cup of sugar equivalent in artificial sweetener (preferably powdered erythritol or liquid sweetener)

Directions:

First, heat oven to a temperature of 375 F.

After which prepare a spring form pan (for me, I prefer to put a piece of parchment paper over the bottom of the pan) there is no need to cut it to size, all you do is just snap it into place when you tighten the sides of the pan. After that, you Butter the sides and bottom of the pan, including parchment and then wrap the outside of the pan in heavy-duty foil to protect it from leaks.

After that, you combine ingredients for crust and then press the mixture into the bottom of your spring form pan.

Then bake for about 8 to 10 minutes until fragrant and beginning to brown.

At this point, remove from oven and then lower oven temperature to 350 F.

In addition, gather ingredients for the filling and then beat cream cheese until fluffy.

After which you scrape sides of bowl and beaters (NOTE: at this point, the mixture will slowly become lighter as you add in the rest of the ingredients, and the denser stuff will cling to the bowl. Remember that if you do not scrape, you will not be able to incorporate the remaining ingredients as well.)

Then add sweetener, vanilla, salt, and 4 of the eggs and then beat well, scrape.

After that, add the other 4 eggs and then beat well, scrape.

This is when add lemon juice, lemon zest, and cream and beat well, scrape, and pour filling mixture into the pan over the crust.

Furthermore, mix together ingredients for topping in a separate bowl and set aside.

After which you place a baking pan large enough to hold your spring form pan into the oven and fill it halfway with boiling water.

After that, place the spring form pan into the baking pan.

Bake for about 61 minutes (give or take 11 to 16 minutes), until the cheesecake is mostly set but is still wobbly in the middle.

Then remove cheesecake from oven, spread the topping over the cheesecake, then bake for an additional 10 minutes.

Finally, cool to room temperature (for about 1 to 2 hours), then you chill completely for several hours before serving.

NUTRITIONAL INFORMATION

Amount per serving: each of 16 serving

Calories: 295

Fiber: 1g

Carbohydrate: 3g

Protein: 7g

Roasted Brussels Sprouts

Ingredients

Salt and Pepper (I find that Brussels sprouts takes more salt than other vegetables, but this is to taste, feel free to always add more)

2 pounds of Brussels sprouts

4 Tablespoons of olive oil (or preferably other fat you want Butter may scorch, but I have heard of people using bacon fat)

Directions:

1. Meanwhile, heat oven to a temperature of 450 degrees F.

2. After which you remove loose or discolored leaves from the outside of the Brussels sprouts, and cut off the brown stem ends.

3. Remember, that most of the sprouts should be cut in half lengthwise and if there are any that are longer than 1½ inches, I suggest you cut those in quarters, if smaller than an inch, leave them whole.

4. After that, toss the Brussels sprouts in the oil and then with the salt and pepper. As for me, I do this right on a baking sheet. (I used a nonstick sheet, but a regular one would probably be okay.) Turn the sprouts so that their flat sides are up.

5. At this point, roast for about 5-6 minutes, or until the underside is just starting to brown after which you turn all the sprouts flat side down (I use tongs for this) and return to the oven.

6. Then roast until the flat side is brown, about another 5 minutes.

7. Finally, check one of the larger ones for doneness by piercing with a sharp knife to make sure it slides in easily.

8. This is when you taste to see if they need more seasoning, and enjoy.

NUTRITIONAL INFORMATION

Amount per serving: each of 6 serving

Calories: 70

Fiber: 3g

Carbohydrate: 4g

Protein: 3g

Fat: 5g

Skillet Chicken Divan

Tips:

1. Feel free to make this low-carb version of chicken divan on the stovetop and run it under the broiler. Or on the other hand, forget the broiler and just serve and eat.

2. In this recipe, feel free to use chopped walnuts or almonds and also milk can be substituted for the soy milk and/or cream, and the proportions of these can be changed as well.

Ingredients

6 cups of cooked chopped broccoli

½ cup of chopped onion

2 Tablespoons of Better than Bouillon and 1 ¼ cups of water, or 1 ¼ cup of chicken broth and salt to taste

1 cup of unsweetened soy milk

2 teaspoons of dried thyme

1 cup of shredded parmesan cheese

5 cups (or so) of chopped cooked chicken

16 oz. of mushrooms (sliced)

1 cup of dry white wine

½ cup of heavy cream

4 teaspoons of low carb thickener such as NOT Starch or 4 tablespoons of whole wheat flour

2 teaspoons of Worcestershire sauce

1 ¼ cups of walnuts, chopped (it will be good if you toast them, but not vital)

Directions:

1. First, you sauté onion and mushrooms in oil for about 4-5 minutes.

2. After which you add wine and boil most of it away.

3. After that, you add thickener and if you are using flour, I suggest you cook for a minute or so before adding the rest of the ingredients.

4. At this point, you add liquids and seasonings.

5. Then you cook, stirring occasionally, for about 2-3 minutes.

6. In addition, you add the rest of the ingredients except the cheese.

7. Finally, you can mix the cheese in or sprinkle it over the top and put the whole thing under the broiler to brown.

NUTRITIONAL INFORMATION

Amount per serving: 1 serving size

Calories: 400

Fiber: 6g

Carbohydrate: 6g

Protein: 31g

St. Louis Barbecue Sauce

Ingredients

½ cup approximately 120 mL water

1/3 cup approximately 80 mL brown sugar

1 tablespoon approximately 15 mL onion powder

1/2 teaspoon approximately 2.5 mL cayenne

2 cups approximately 475 mL ketchup

1/3 cup approximately 80 mL apple cider vinegar

2 tablespoons approximately 30 mL yellow mustard

1 tablespoon approximately 15 mL garlic powder

Directions:

1. First, you combine all ingredients in a saucepan over a low heat.

2. After which you stir occasionally and simmer for about 20 minutes. Remember that the sauce should be thin, but not watery.

3. After that, you allow to cool.

4. Finally, you store in an airtight container and refrigerate.

Note: that sauce is better if allow to sit for a day.

Stir-Fried Kung Pao Chicken with Chili Peppers

Tips:

This recipe is a healthier version of traditional "Kung Pao Chicken", here the chicken is stir-fried instead of deep-fried, reducing the fat content their in.

Ingredients

4 boneless, skinless chicken breasts (about 14 to 16 ounces each)

Marinade:

4 teaspoons Chinese rice wine (or preferably dry sherry)

3 teaspoons of cornstarch

4 teaspoons of soy sauce

2 teaspoons of sesame oil

Sauce:

2 tablespoons of Chinese rice wine (or preferably dry sherry)

2 teaspoons of sugar

4 tablespoons of dark soy sauce

Other:

4 cloves garlic

8 tablespoons of oil for stir-frying, or as needed

Few drops of sesame oil (it is optional)

16 small dried red chili peppers

4 green onions (spring onions, scallions)

2 teaspoons of Szechuan peppercorn (it is optional)

1 cup of peanuts (or preferably cashews)

Directions:

1. First, you cut the chicken into 1-inch cubes.

2. After, which you combine with the marinade ingredients, adding the cornstarch last.

3. After that, marinate the chicken for about 25 minutes.

4. At this point, that the chicken is marinating, you prepare the sauce and vegetables.

5. Then combine the dark soy sauce, rice wine, and sugar and then set aside.

6. In addition, cut the chilies in half so that they are approximately the same size as the chicken cubes and then remove the seeds.

7. This is when you peel and finely chop the garlic.

8. After which you cut the green onion on the diagonal into thirds.

9. Furthermore, heat the wok over medium-high to high heat.

10. After that, add 4 tablespoons of oil and then when the oil is hot, add the chicken.

11. Then stir-fry until it turns white and is 80 percent cooked after which you remove from the wok.

12. This is when add 4 tablespoons of oil and when the oil is hot, you add the garlic and stir-fry for about 30 seconds until aromatic.

13. At this point, add the chili peppers and the Szechuan peppercorn if you using it after that you stir-fry briefly until they turn dark red.

14. Finally, add the sauce to the wok and then bring to a boil.

15. Add the chicken back into the pan, stir in the peanuts and the green onion and then remove from the heat and stir in the sesame oil.

16. Make sure you serve hot.

Strawberry Chicken Salad

Tips:

1. This recipe is quite lovely, light, and different.

2. After which you dress with strawberry vinaigrette dressing and have a real treat on a hot summer night.

Ingredients

16 cups of lettuce, spinach, and/or arugula (fill a 2-quart mixing bowl)

4 oz. feta cheese, crumbled (Parmesan is also good)

1 lb. boneless skinless chicken breast (grilled or broiled)

4 cups of sliced strawberries

½ cup of sliced or preferably slivered toasted almonds (toasted pine nuts or sunflower seeds are also nice)

Directions:

1. First, toss the greens with about ½ cup of strawberry vinaigrette or better still other oil and vinegar type salad dressing.

2. Then arrange the rest of the ingredients on top of the greens.

NOTE: For meal-sized salads, I suggest you distribute between two plates or bowls.

NUTRITIONAL INFORMATION (without dressing)

Amount per serving: 1 serving size

Calories: 319

Fiber: 5.5g

Carbohydrate: 9g

Protein: 35g

NUTRITIONAL INFORMATION (with strawberry vinaigrette)

Amount per serving: 1 serving size

Calories: 442

Fiber: 5.5g

Carbohydrate: 9g

Protein: 35g

Strawberry Vinaigrette

Tips:

1. This dressing is quite good on any green salad, if you want something different.

2. I cherish it better with Strawberry Chicken Salad, which is a meal salad with greens, strawberries, and chicken.

Ingredients

1 cup of sliced strawberries

4 tablespoons of red wine vinegar (or preferably balsamic, but carb count vary, so be careful)

Sweetener to taste (it depends on sweetness of strawberries; you might not need it)

1 cup of olive oil

2 teaspoons of mustard

Salt and pepper to taste

Directions:

1. First, you puree strawberries in a blender or food processor.

2. After which you add vinegar, mustard, and seasonings.

3. After that, you blend, then add olive oil and then blend until creamy.

4. Then you taste and adjust seasonings.

5. Note: it makes 8 servings of about 4 tablespoons each.

NUTRITIONAL INFORMATION

Amount per serving: 1 serving size

Calories: 123

Carbohydrate: 0.5g

Almond Spice Cookies

Ingredients

2 cups almond meal (with skins works fine)

1½ Tablespoons apple pie spice, or 1 teaspoon cinnamon, ½ teaspoon nutmeg, and a pinch of cloves

½ teaspoon salt

½ cup sugar equivalent in artificial sweetener (zero carb preferred, such as liquid sweetener)

1 large egg

½ teaspoon vanilla

1 packet artificial sweetener (to sprinkle on top)

Sliced almonds (optional)

Directions:

1. First, heat oven to a temperature of 325 F.

2. After which you combine all dry ingredients (a whisk works well).

3. After that, add the wet ingredients, and combine well, until mixture has formed a large ball.

4. At this point, it will form balls about one inch in size.

5. Then flatten with hands or a spoon to about ¼ inch thickness.

6. Finally, sprinkle powdered sweetener on the tops and then place on baking sheet covered with parchment or silicon mat. (In the other hand, you grease the baking sheet.)

7. This is when you top with sliced almonds, if you wish.

8. Finally, bake for about 10 to 12 minutes, or until cookies are slightly brown on bottom.

NUTRITIONAL INFORMATION

Amount per serving: 1 cookie

Calories: 50

Fiber: 1g

Carbohydrate: 0.5g

Protein: 2g

Easy Baby Back Ribs

Tips:

Now you can have a new version of finger-licking baby back ribs that are just as succulent and sugar free.

Ingredients

Salt and spices

Sugar-free BBQ sauce

Baby Back Ribs (feel free to use as many racks as you want)

Diet cola

Directions:

There are two phases to making baby back ribs as follows:

1. The first is a long slow braise (i.e. cooking in a little liquid) this is to dissolve all the connective tissue in the ribs (smoking accomplishes the same thing) Otherwise they would be very tough.

2. However, this can be accomplished in the oven or better still the crockpot, but in the heat of the summer I prefer to keep the whole process outside.

The second phase is the grilling, which is quick. First, you sprinkle the ribs with salt, pepper, garlic powder, and chili powder.

(**NOTE:** If you have a special rub you like that doesn't have sugar content in it, by all means use that.) I recommend Cajun and Old Bay which are also good.

After which, you pat the spices in, and put ribs in the refrigerator for at least an hour.

After that, you wrap the ribs loosely in heavy-duty foil, but seal the sides, but if you are using the slow cooker/crock pot, omit this step.

At this point, you pour half a can of diet cola into the packet (or preferably crock pot).

NOTE: If you don't like any sweetness in your ribs, or if you just prefer not to use soda, I recommend white wine, or better still white wine with a few drops of sweetener.

Then you seal the top of the ribs. This is when you put the ribs in a covered grill with low heat (either charcoal or gas), or better still on a baking sheet in the oven.

Directions on Cooking times:

1. I was meant to understand that 2 and ½ hours at about 250 F. works very well, but if you don't have that much time on your hand, I will suggest 1 and ½ hours at 350 F. also works.

2. However, in the crockpot, you cook for about 8 hours or so on low. For every 45-60 minutes, I suggest you add liquid if needed (note that the amount of juice in the ribs does vary), and turn the ribs over. Finally, you open the foil, and brush the ribs with sugar-free BBQ sauce.

3. Make sure you grill on medium to medium-high heat for about 10 minutes on each side and then serve with sauce to dunk ribs in.

Cranberry Walnut Cookies

Tips:

This cookie makes a nice Christmas cookie and it is absolutely Sugar-free, low-carb, and gluten-free.

Ingredients

2 cups of whey protein powder

8 oz. of cream cheese (feel free to use low fat)

Sugar substitute equal to 2 and 1 cups of sugar

2 teaspoons of baking soda

2 cups of whole cranberries (fresh or frozen and with no sugar added)

2 and 1 cups of almond meal

1 cup (one stick) of butter

4 eggs

2 teaspoons of cinnamon

2 teaspoons of salt

1 ¼ cups of chopped walnuts

Notes on Special Ingredients to use:

A combination of almond meal and whey protein powder takes the place of flour and if you use a flavored protein powder, I suggest you will probably want to cut down the amount of sweetener in the recipe. As for me, I used Designer Brand Vanilla Praline, which have artificial flavorings in it. Nevertheless, if I did not use the flavored powder, I'd be more inclined to add a little intense black molasses, which has approximately 4 to 5 grams of carbohydrate per teaspoon (I used liquid sucralose).

Directions:

1. Meanwhile, you heat oven to a temperature of 375 F.

2. After which you cream butter and cream cheese together until fluffy.

3. After that, you add sweetener, cinnamon, and salt, and beat again.

4. In addition, you add eggs, and beat until combined after which you add almond meal, protein powder, and baking soda and combine well.

5. At this point, you mix in cranberries and walnuts.

6. Then you drop by rounded spoonful onto an ungreased cookie sheet, or preferably one covered with a silicone mat.

7. The size is up to you, but I advise you avoid very large cookies.

8. This is when you bake for about 7 to 9 minutes, until top is just browning.

9. Finally, you cool completely before eating, trust me they are so much better after they are cool.

10. Make sure you store in a sealed container.

NUTRITIONAL INFORMATION

Amount per serving: 32 cookies

Calories: 94

Fiber: 1g

Carbohydrate: 1g

Protein: 4g

Sugar-Free Chocolate Pecan Torte

Ingredients

2/3 cup of cocoa

½ teaspoon of salt

1 cup (I stick) of butter, melted

½ cup of erythritol (it is optional)

1 cup of water

4 cups of pecans (make sure you don't use salted pecans!)

2 teaspoons of baking powder

8 eggs

2 teaspoons of vanilla

Artificial sweetener equivalent to 2 cups of sugar (I used zero-carb liquid sweeteners which was nice)

Directions:

1. First, you heat oven to a temperature of 350 F.

2. After which you grease an 8 or 9" round pan or spring form pan.

3. After that, you process pecans in food processor and then pulse until they are meal (note that they won't get quite as small as corn meal).

4. Then you add the rest of the dry ingredients and pulse again (note: I use more erythritol and is even better).

5. At this point, you add the wet ingredients and process until well-blended.

6. In addition, you pour into pan and bake. Remember, the exact time will vary with the pan and I suggest you start checking at about 25 minutes until toothpick inserted in center comes out clean.

7. Finally, you cut when cool and if you wish, serve with homemade whipped cream and/or chocolate sauce.

NUTRITIONAL INFORMATION

Amount per serving: each of 8 servings

Calories: 334

Fiber: 4g

Carbohydrate: 2g

Protein: 6g

Peanut Butter Cups (Low Carb)

Notes:

1. However, these sugar-free, low-carb recipe cups are far better than any "diet candy" you can buy in a store.

2. In the other hand, you need a mini-muffin pan, preferably non-stick.

Ingredients

½ cup of heavy cream

Artificial sweetener equal to 2 cups of sugar (preferably, concentrated liquid Splenda)

2 teaspoons of vanilla

10 oz. of unsweetened chocolate

1 ¼ cups of powdered erythritol

½ teaspoons of salt

Ingredients for the filling:

2 cups of almond meal/flour

Dash of salt

1 cup of peanut butter

Artificial sweetener equal to 2 cups of sugar (preferably liquid sucralose)

Notes on the Methods and Ingredients:

It is essential not to overheat the chocolate, because chocolate melts at a little below body temperature. However, you don't need much heat. There are many ways you can melt chocolate, first, you can pour boiling water over it and then pour it off, you can heat the cream and then turn off the heat, or preferably use any method of your choice. Note that if you heat it too much it will separate and if this happens, I suggest you mix in a bunch of peanut butter and cut it into squares when cool. Or pour off the cocoa butter and put nuts in it along with the other ingredients for the chocolate outside, and it will be a very good fudge.

I recommend you use Hershey unsweetened chocolate because I figured it being readily available and if you use a higher-quality chocolate like Ghirardelli you will need more sweetener as much as half again as much of the zero-carb sweetener.

Directions:

1. First, you heat cream and the rest of ingredients and then turn off heat and add chocolate.

2. In the other hand, if you're melting it in the cream, I suggest you let stand until chocolate is melted -stir once in a while. Once it is all melted, mixture will be fairly thick. I will recommend you adjust sweetener to taste.

3. At this point, while the cream is heating and chocolate melting, I suggest you mix up the filling.

4. However, if it is too sticky, I suggest you put a little more almond flour or erythritol into it and then adjust sweetness (and possibly salt level) to taste.

5. After which you put heaping tablespoons or globs of the chocolate the size of a walnut into the mini muffin tin and then if it is thick enough you can sort of push out a place in the center and make the chocolate even around the sides. In addition, if it is not yet thick enough for this, don't worry, the peanut butter will push it up the sides.

6. After that, you form the peanut butter into smaller globs/balls and then push them into the chocolate, including pushing the top so it's flat.

7. Then chill the whole thing in the refrigerator for half an hour or so.

8. This is when you remove from fridge and run hot water over the bottom of the pan for just a few seconds.

9. Finally, take a thin knife and insert it at the edge of a cup.

10. Make sure you turn the whole thing a bit - then you know you can easily pop it out and if it doesn't work right away, I suggest you give it a few seconds so that the heat can penetrate, or it may need another shot of heat.

NUTRITIONAL INFORMATION

Amount per serving: 1 serving size

Calories: 125

Fiber: 2g

Carbohydrate: 2.5g

Fresh Berry Pie (Sugar-Free)

Ingredients

2 quarts (8 cups) of fresh blackberries

1 ¼ cups of water

2 Tablespoons of butter (it is optional, but recommended)

For example, you could use 1 ¼ cups of Da Vinci's Simple Syrup instead of water

2 almond pie crust (baked)

Dash of salt

8 teaspoons of corn starch

Sugar substitute to taste (about 1 ¼ cups - liquid form of Splenda preferred)

Directions:

1. First, you mix the water, one cup of berries, salt, and sweetener in a saucepan (make sure it is big enough to eventually hold all the berries).

2. After which you bring the mixture to a boil and cook for about 2 to 3 minutes (berries should be softening and the liquid berry-colored).

3. After that, you whisk cornstarch into mixture (Make sure it is fully dissolved).

4. At this point, you cook until mixture darkens and clarifies (in other words, most of the lightness from the cornstarch goes away).

5. Then you add butter, and stir until melted.

6. In addition, you add the rest of the berries, and stir until coated with the glaze.

7. Finally, you pour into baked shell and chill. Serving suggestion:

Feel free to top with whipped cream flavored with a bit of vanilla and sweetener.

NUTRITIONAL INFORMATION

Amount per serving: 1 serving size

Calories: 189

Fiber: 6g

Carbohydrate: 5.5g

MY WHOLE 30 DIET RECIPES

Protein: 5g

Super-Easy Guacamole

Ingredients

About ½ teaspoon of salt per avocado

About 1 ¼ teaspoons of garlic powder per avocado

Chopped cilantro, chopped onion (it is optional)

Avocados (number depends on the size of the crowd)

About 4 tablespoons of salsa per avocado

About 1 teaspoon of lemon or preferably lime juice per avocado

Directions:

1. First, you cut the avocados in half, squeeze out the pit (you should squeeze gently till it pops out) and then scoop the fruit into a bowl.

2. After which you add the salt, juice, salsa, and garlic powder and then mash it together with a fork (I prefer to leave some chunks).

3. After that, you taste and if you can't taste the avocado much, I suggest you add a bit of salt. In the other hand, if you find it a little flat, dribble a little juice in and if not spicy enough, add a little salsa.

4. However, I recommend you try more garlic powder to see how that changes it and then play with it and you will find your "ideal guac balance point" (this is the secret to excellent guacamole)

5. At this point, you stir in cilantro and onion at the end if you want to. I do the cilantro, but not always.

6. Finally, by the third time you do this, I don't think you will bother to measure, you'll just put the ingredients in and start tasting. Note: for a healthy low-carb snack, I suggest you serve with vegetables such as pepper strips, jicama and cucumber.

NUTRITIONAL INFORMATION

Amount per serving: 1 serving size

Calories: 227

Fiber: 12g

Carbohydrate: 3g

Protein: 2.5g

Piquant Sauce for Meatloaf (Low Carb)

Ingredients

2 teaspoons of dry mustard

Sweetener to taste - I prefer 2 Tablespoons worth, but have seen recipes with up to 6 tablespoons of sugar

½ cup of low carb ketchup

½ teaspoon of nutmeg

Directions:

1. First, you mix all ingredients together (as for me, I usually put the ketchup in a glass cup measure and then add the rest).

2. **NOTE** that one Tablespoon carb per tablespoon for the ketchup, the whole recipe summed up to 5 grams of carbohydrate.

Chengdu Chicken

Ingredients

4 large or 6 small boneless, skinless chicken breasts (about 28 - 32 ounces total)

Marinade:

2 tablespoons of rice wine (or dry sherry)

6 teaspoons of cornstarch

2 tablespoons of soy sauce

Pinches of black pepper (it is optional)

½ teaspoon of sesame oil

Sauce:

2 tablespoons of soy sauce

3 teaspoons of cornstarch mixed in 4 tablespoons of water

2 tablespoons of rice wine (or dry sherry)

4 teaspoons of red wine vinegar or rice vinegar (preferably red rice vinegar)

2 teaspoons of sugar

Other:

2 garlic clove

1 bunch of spinach

2 tablespoons of hot bean paste

10 tablespoons of vegetable oil for stir-frying, or as needed

2 green onions (preferably spring onion, scallion)

4 slices of ginger

Salt to season spinach

1 teaspoon of sesame oil (or to taste)

2 teaspoons of freshly ground Szechuan pepper (or coriander)

Directions:

1. First, you wash the chicken breasts and pat dry.

2. After which you remove any fat and cut into strips and then into 1-inch cubes. After that, you add the marinade ingredients, adding the cornstarch last.
3. At this point, you marinate the chicken for about 20 minutes and while the chicken is marinating, prepare the sauce and the vegetables.
4. Then you combine the rice wine or dry sherry, soy sauce, vinegar and sugar.
5. In addition, dissolve the cornstarch into the water in a separate small bowl and set aside. This is when you wash the green onion and chop into small pieces.
6. Furthermore, you smash and peel the garlic.
7. After which you chop the garlic and ginger and then wash and drain the spinach. Heat the wok and when the wok is hot, you add 2 tablespoons of oil.
8. Add the spinach and sprinkle a bit of salt of top and as soon as the spinach wilts (a few seconds), you remove it and set aside. This is when you clean out the wok and heat 8 tablespoons oil and then add the chicken cubes, stir-frying continually to keep them from sticking.
9. Once the chicken changes color and is nearly 80 percent cooked, I suggest you remove it from the wok and then leave 4 tablespoons of oil in the wok. At this point, you add the garlic, ginger and hot bean paste to the wok, after which you stir-fry briefly until fragrant (about 30 seconds).
10. Add the chicken back into the wok and mix with the hot bean paste, after that, you push the chicken back up to the sides and add the sauce mixture in the middle.
11. This moment you give the cornstarch and water mixture a quick re-stir and mix it in the sauce, stirring quickly to thicken. Finally, you mix the sauce with the chicken and then stir in the green onion and sesame oil.
12. Make sure you sprinkle the freshly ground Szechuan pepper over top and then serve with the stir-fried spinach.

Terri's Tofu Scramble

Ingredients

4 tablespoons of nutritional yeast

4 teaspoons of low sodium tamari or soy sauce

¼ teaspoons of black pepper

1 bell pepper (diced)

2 tablespoons of canola oil (or other mild-flavored oil of your choice)

2 lbs. of firm tofu

1 teaspoon of turmeric

¼ teaspoon of cayenne pepper

2 stalk broccoli (chopped very well)

1 onion (diced)

4 slices of Fakin' Bacon (preferably, tempeh bacon substitute), chopped small

Directions:

1. First, you drain the tofu and then cut it into pieces and pour it into a small mixing bowl.

2. After that, you add the turmeric, nutritional yeast, cayenne, tamari/soy sauce and pepper and with a fork, mash it all up until there are no big chunks.

3. Feel free to use it right away, but for the best flavor, I suggest you cover with plastic wrap and refrigerate overnight.

4. At this point, you heat the canola oil in a frying pan and add the Fakin' Bacon.

5. Then you sauté until the pieces are brown and crispy.

6. In addition, you add the vegetables and stir-fry until they are tender.

7. Finally, you add the tofu mixture and stir-fry until the tofu is heated through.

NUTRITIONAL INFORMATION

Amount per serving: each of 4 servings

Calories: 250

Fiber: 4g

Carbohydrate: 9g

Protein: 24g

Tuna Walnut Salad

Note:

This recipe is tastier when the walnuts are toasted.

Ingredients

2 large stalk celery (chopped finely)

Pinches of cinnamon

Salt and pepper to taste

2 (6 oz. each) can tuna fish

½ cup of chopped walnuts (toasted if you wish, it really is much better)

6 tablespoons of mayonnaise (or to taste)

Directions:

All you do is to mix it all up.

NUTRITIONAL INFORMATION

Amount per serving: each of 2 serving

Calories: 350

Fiber: 1.5g

Carbohydrate: 1.5g

Protein: 23g

Tzatziki with Mint - Cucumber Yogurt Sauce or Side Dish

Ingredients

4 cups (16 oz. each) of plain yogurt (strained or Greek style)

Salt

2 cucumbers (preferably English or seedless)

8 cloves garlic (minced)

½ - 2/3 cup of chopped mint leaves

Directions:

Remember, that if cucumber is "regular" (not English), you might want to take the seeds out, because that section of the cucumber is pretty watery. I prefer using English or seedless cucumber for tzatziki.

1. First, you grate the cucumber and put it in a strainer.

2. After which you sprinkle a little salt over it and mix in.

3. After that, you let it drain for a while (at least 10 minutes) then squeeze it down to get as much juice out as possible.

4. At this point, you mix with the rest of the ingredients.

5. Finally, you drizzle some olive oil over the top if you wish.

NUTRITIONAL INFORMATION

Amount per serving: each of 10 serving

Calories: 53

Carbohydrate: 3.5g

Vegan Curried Tofu and Walnut Salad Recipe

Note:

This recipe is full of tantalizing spices and textures and is similar to an egg salad.

Make sure you serve on a bed of green lettuce, or make tofu salad sandwiches.

Ingredients

2/3 cup of prepared Italian salad dressing

½ teaspoon of pepper

2 onions (diced)

Lettuce

2 pounds of firm or extra firm tofu (well-pressed)

2 tablespoons of curry powder

½ teaspoon of salt

6 stalks celery (diced)

2 cups of walnuts (chopped)

Directions:

1. First, you cut tofu into ½ inch cubes.

2. After which you pour the salad dressing in a large mixing bowl over the tofu and mix.

3. After that, you add remaining ingredients, except for the lettuce and combine well.

4. At this point, you refrigerate before serving for at least one hour to allow flavors to combine.

5. Then you serve on a bed of green lettuce.

6. Enjoy!

Sugar-Free Instant Pumpkin Pudding

NOTE:

1. This recipe is very nutritious and any "milky" liquid work fine (as for me, I used unsweetened soy milk for a low carb count, but milk, unsweetened almond milk, or water mixed with cream, 3 to one is good) all work.

2. Make sure you adjust the carb counts accordingly.

Ingredients

4 cups of unsweetened soy milk

½ teaspoon of nutmeg

If using butterscotch, add 2 teaspoons of vanilla

2 (15-16 oz.) of can pumpkin

3 teaspoons of cinnamon

½ teaspoon of ginger

2 boxes of instant (no-cook) sugar-free butterscotch (or preferable vanilla pudding, 12 serving size)

Directions:

1. First, you whisk together the pumpkin, spices, and half the milk in a medium bowl.

2. After which while whisking, you add the pudding mix and the rest of the milk.

3. After that, you whisk well to fully combine (You can also use a stick blender.).

4. At this point, the pudding will continue to thicken a little over time.

5. Feel free to add more liquid and/or spices for the consistency and flavor of your choice.

Directions for Serving Suggestion:

You can top with toasted pecans.

NUTRITIONAL INFORMATION

Amount per serving: 1 serving size

Calories: 62

Fiber: 3g

Fat: 1.4

Carbohydrate: 8g

Protein: 4g

Warm Spinach Salad with Hot Bacon Dressing

Tips:

1. This version of recipe can easily be made into a meal by adding chopped cooked chicken, turkey, or even fish or tofu.

2. Remember that chopped egg is also a classic option and if you wish for more vegetables, mushrooms and red pepper work especially well.

Ingredients

8 pieces of thick-cut bacon or preferably 12 pieces thin cut (approximately 150 grams), chopped

2 cloves garlic

Pinches of salt

4 teaspoons of worth sugar substitute

2 package of baby spinach (about 18-20 oz.) or that much washed spinach leaves

½ cup of minced onion

4 Tablespoons of cider vinegar (or preferably the same amount as the bacon fat)

4 pinches of pepper

Directions:

1. First, you put the spinach (and other vegetables if you like) in a large bowl.

2. Remember that the spinach will shrink down some in the hot dressing, but you need room to work.

3. After which you chop the bacon and fry until crisp.

4. Then you remove with slotted spoon and drain on paper towels.

5. On the other hand, if you like a lightly dressed salad, I suggest you leave about 4 Tablespoons of the bacon fat in the pan and if you wish for more dressing, leave fatter and then balance it with more vinegar and a bit more sweetener. (I like it because this dressing is a sweet and sour sort of thing.)

6. At this point, you cook the onion in the fat for about 2-3 minutes, and then add the garlic.

7. After that, you cook for another 15-30 seconds or until it is starting to be fragrant (note: be careful not to brown the garlic or it will get bitter).

8. In addition, you add the vinegar, and scrape up the brown bits in the pan (Note that the vinegar will seem potent, but it mellows quickly with the heat and sweetener).

9. This is when you add the salt, pepper, and sweetener.

10. After which you stir to dissolve, and pour the dressing over the spinach.

11. Then you toss the spinach (tongs work well) until coated.

12. Finally, you transfer to individual plates or bowls and top with bacon bits and other toppings as desired.

13. Makes three ample servings as a side dish.

NUTRITIONAL INFORMATION

Amount per serving: 1 serving size

Calories: 194

Fiber: 2.5g

Carbohydrate: 3.5g

Protein: 9g

Watermelon Salad with Cucumber and Mint

Note:

1. This recipe is so delicious, refreshing, and easy to make and because it is different, people like it at potlucks, it can be easily adjusted to make many portions or a few.

2. In addition, the saltiness of the cheese makes a surprisingly delicious contrast to the watermelon.

Ingredients

4 cups of cucumber, chopped

2/3 cup of crumbled feta cheese

4 cups of watermelon, chopped

½ cup of fresh mint, minced

Directions:

1. First, you mix watermelon, cucumber, and most of the mint and cheese together.

2. After which you sprinkle remaining mint and cheese on top.

3. Then you garnish with whole mint leaves if desired.

NUTRITIONAL INFORMATION

Amount per serving: each of 8 serving

Calories: 33

Fiber: 1g

Carbohydrate: 3.5g

Protein: 1g

Blueberry Cream Cheese Coffeecakes

NOTE:

1. This delicious low-carb recipe is very filling, since it is made with almond meal.

2. If you do not like cream cheese, I suggest you can leave out that layer, or use less cream cheese.

3. It is also delicious with raspberries; wish you gave it a trial.

Ingredients:

3 cups of sugar substitute (preferably liquid or powdered)

2 teaspoons of baking powder

½ cup of butter, about 8 tablespoons (chilled and cut into small bits)

4 teaspoons of vanilla extract (or 2 teaspoons each of vanilla and almond extracts)

12 oz. of cream cheese

2 cups of fresh or frozen blueberries or raspberries (but not thawed)

6 cups of almond meal

6 eggs

1 teaspoon of baking soda

1 cup of sour cream

Salt to taste

4 Tablespoons of oil

Directions:

Tips:

1. First, you preheat oven to a temperature of 350°.

2. After which you butter or oil 9X9 inch pan (Note: cooking spray is fine).

3. This recipe is prepared in 3 consecutive layers:

4. If you are using a standing mixer, I suggest you feel free to use the same bowl if you make the layers in the order listed - just remove them to separate bowls until ready to assemble.

Directions for the Streusel Topping:

1. First, you mix 2 cups of the almond meal, 2-teaspoons of cinnamon, 1 cup of sweetener, a pinch of salt and the 8 Tablespoons of butter.

2. The whisk type attachment on a standing mixer works well - you want the mixture to stay crumbly. Feel free to use a pastry blender, knives - whatever works.

3. Nevertheless, if it clumps together, do not worry all you do is to just crumble it over the top when the time comes.

4. At this point, use powdered sweetener, preferable liquid sucralose (zero-carb) works fine.

Direction for the Cream Cheese Layer:

1. First, you mix cream cheese, 2 eggs, and ½-cup sweetener.

2. If you want a thinner layer of cream cheese, I suggest you use 8 oz. instead of 12.

Directions for the Cake layer:

3. First, you mix all the dry ingredients ranging from: baking powder, 4 cups of almond flour, baking soda, teaspoon salt, 1 ¼ cup of sweetener if you are using a powder and 1-teaspoon of cinnamon.

4. After which you add the oil, extracts, sour cream, liquid sweetener, and 2 eggs and mix well.

5. Then you add 3 Tablespoons of water (depending on the consistency).

6. If you want the batter to be thick enough to support the rest of it, but not too gloppy, I suggest you spread it easily on the pan.

Direction for Assembling:

1. First, you spread the cake layer in the pan, and spread the cream cheese on top.

2. After which you sprinkle the blueberries on the cream cheese and the streusel on the top of that.

3. Finally, you bake for about ½ an hour, or until toothpick not inserted into a berry comes out clean.

4. It should be about 155° F. in the center, if you using a thermometer to check.

5. Then you cool and slice (It is filling, so I prefer cutting it into 16 pieces).

Nutritional value:

Amount per serving

Calories: 217

Fat: g

Carb: 3g

Protein: 6g

Dietary fiber: 2.5g

"Doughnut" Muffins

NOTE:

1. This recipe is one from a few recipes for which I use powdered Splenda for (for the topping).

2. In this recipe, you do not end up using much per muffin, but you need enough to dip the tops.

3. I suggest you save the rest for cinnamon toast made with flax meal bread.

Ingredients:

2 cups of almond meal

½ teaspoon of salt

2 teaspoons of cinnamon

1 cup of (2 sticks) butter, melted

1 cup and 2 Tablespoons of water

2 cups of flax meal

2 Tablespoons of baking powder

2 ½ teaspoons of nutmeg

4 eggs (beaten)

Artificial sweetener (2-cup equivalent - zero carb preferable liquid)

Topping:

2 t cinnamon

2 T melted butter

1/2 cup equivalent powdered artificial sweetener

Tips:

1. You are to makes 24 regular-size muffins. Preheat oven to a temperature of 350 degrees F.

2. After which you butter muffin pans.

Directions:

1. First, mix dry ingredients well (**Note:** exclude those used for topping).

2. After which you add beaten eggs, melted butter, water, and sweetener to the dry mixture.

3. Then mix well.

4. Furthermore, fill muffin cups a bit more than ½ ways with the mixture.

5. After which you bake for approximately 20 minutes, until tops are golden brown.

6. Then allow muffins to cool in pan for a few minutes, before you remove.

7. In addition, mix the cinnamon and powdered sweetener for the topping in a clean bowl.

8. Then when the muffins are cool enough to handle, I suggest you dip the tops in the melted butter you allocated for the topping, followed by the sweetener/cinnamon mixture.

Directions for the Buttermilk Version:

1. First, you switch out 1-cup buttermilk for the same amount of water.

2. After which you substitute 2 teaspoons baking soda and 2 teaspoons baking powder for the baking powder in the regular recipe.

3. Remember that this variation adds ½ a gram of carb to each muffin.

Nutritional value: per muffin

Amount per serving

Carb: 1.5g

Dietary fiber: 4g

Gnocchi

Ingredients:

2 (16 oz.) container whole milk ricotta cheese

2 teaspoons of onion powder

1 teaspoon of pepper

2 (10 oz.) package frozen chopped spinach, thawed and well-drained

2 teaspoons of garlic powder

1 teaspoon of salt

2 pinch of nutmeg

2 cups of Carb Counter Instant Mashers

2 eggs

Directions:

1. First, you squeeze the spinach to make sure the excess water is out of it.

2. After which you put spinach in food processor with steel blade.

3. Then you process in a few seconds to break down the spinach.

4. Furthermore, you add ricotta cheese, salt and spices.

5. After which you process with the spinach.

6. At this point, you taste for flavor and salt content.

7. Then you add egg and process to blend.

8. In addition, you add Instant Mashers ½ cup at a time, and process until blended.

9. It depend on the amount of liquid in the ricotta and spinach, you might need a little more or less that your choice to make.

10. For instance, you might want the mixture to be stiff enough to roll into small balls that keep their shape.

11. After which you roll the mixture into small balls, ¾ inch to 1 inch in diameter.

12. Then you gently squeeze between thumb and forefinger making indentations on both sides.

Directions for microwave method

1. First, you put on microwave-safe plates.

2. You might want to make 3 or 4 plates; make sure not to crowd them.

Directions for boiling method

First, you put on plates or baking sheet to be put into freezer or refrigerator.

Directions for microwave method:

1. Make sure you cover plate with plastic wrap or waxed paper.

2. Then you microwave on high for approximately 60-90 seconds.

3. Furthermore, you rearrange so the center gets enough heat, then you cook for another minute.

Note: When hot and firm (but not hard), you know they are okay.

Directions for Boiling Method:

1. Make sure the Gnocchi is chilled for this to work properly

2. Place for ½ hour in the freezer or 2 hours in the refrigerator.

3. Make sure they do not warm up in the kitchen before putting them in the water or they will be too soft.

4. Remember to bring at least 3 quarts of salted water just to a boil in a large pot.

5. **Note:** if you use rolling boil it will start to break the gnocchi apart.

6. Just a simmer is better.

7. After which you put them into the water, 10 or 12 at a time.

8. When they rise to the surface, you know they are okay.

9. At this point, you remove and drain well.

10. It will take a minute or so.

11. This will be softer than using the microwave method, but note that if they go in cold, they will hold together.

12. Makes 4 servings as a main course, 6 as a side dish. You can use any sauce you want. We like garlic and butter, tomato sauce, or pesto.

Nutritional value: per serving

Amount per serving

Calories: 150

Carb: 5.5g

Protein: 22g

Dietary fiber: 4g

Biscotti

Tips:

1. Meanwhile, you heat oven to a temperature of 350 F.

2. After which you cover a 10" X 15" baking sheet with parchment paper or a silicone mat, and grease lightly with butter or oil.

Notes:

1. If you want something sweet, yet sugar-free, to dunk in your coffee or tea? These low-carb biscotti might just be what you looking!

I made two variations here:

Basic almond biscotti

Chocolate chip biscotti.

2. Feel free to use any sugar-free chocolate; I suggest you use Choco Perfection Bars, which sweetened with erythritol instead of the more commonly used maltitol.

3. For the chocolate chip biscotti, I suggest you consider reversing the amounts of the vanilla and almond extracts if that would be more to your taste. Another variation is for you to substitute a quarter cup of unsweetened dried blueberries for the chocolate. It will add about ½ a gram of carb per cookie.

Ingredients:

6 cups of almond meal

½-teaspoon of salt

4 teaspoons of almond extract

Ingredient for chocolate chip biscotti:

4 Chocó Perfection Bars (or two 100 grams of other sugar-free chocolate, chocolate chips, etc.)

2 sticks (a cup) of butter at room temperature

2 tablespoons of baking powder

4 eggs

2 teaspoons of vanilla extract

Sugar substitute equal to one cup sugar. Note: zero-carb liquid is preferred -- I used 24 drops of a concentrated form of sucralose (see note)

Directions:

1. First, you mix butter, almond meal, baking powder, and salt together in a large mixing bowl.

2. After which you beat until fully combined (it should glom together).

3. Then you add wet ingredients such as eggs, extracts, and sugar substitute.

4. Furthermore, you beat until well combined.

5. After which you batter will be a bit stiff. (Note: I suggest you developed this recipe using the concentrated liquid sucralose).

6. If you are using a powdered type of sugar substitute, I suggest you add it with the almond meal at the beginning, and make sure to add the carbs to the total.

7. Then you let batter sit for about 5 minutes or so; the almond meal will absorb some of the remaining liquid.

8. Make sure it forms a soft, but workable dough.

Tips for the Chocolate Chip Variation:

1. If you are making the chocolate chip type, I suggest this is a good time to chop the chocolate (i.e. if not already in chip form).

2. You use either a sharp knife or a food processor.

3. If you using a food processor, I advise you pulse carefully if you're too aggressive, this is because much of the chocolate will end up pulverized, and won't have the same effect.

4. In addition, you turn the dough onto the baking sheet and form it into a rectangle about 1/2" - 3/4" high, 5 inches wide, and 14 inches long.

5. After which you bake until very lightly browned on top at about 22-25 minutes.

6. Then you remove from the oven and turn the oven down to 325.

7. Allow the cookies cool for about 5-10 minutes, then cut into slices about 3/4 inch wide.

8. At this point, you lay the slices on their sides, and return to the oven for about 15 minutes, until the sides become lightly browned.

9. After which you can leave the biscotti long.

10. Then you cut them in half, and then each one is a serving.

Finally, you let to cool completely before serving or storing in an airtight container.

Nutritional value: per 36 servings

Amount per serving

Calories: 73

Carb: 1g

Protein: 2g

Dietary fiber: 1g

Zucchini "Pasta"

Tips:

1. Remember that the noodles can be more like fettuccine or linguine, it all depends on how wide you cut them.

2. I suggest you try this recipe with pesto sauce as a side dish.

Ingredients:

Salt to taste

Zucchini

Directions:

1. First, you Use a vegetable peeler, peel strips off zucchini, working your way around the squash.

2. They can be as narrow or as wide as you prefer.

3. Make sure you keep going until you reach the seeds (a few seeds will not matter, though you will not want it seedy).

4. Remember, that you can also use a mandolin for this.

5. After which you put the zucchini strips in a colander or strainer.

6. Then you sprinkle a liberal amount of salt over them, and toss to coat.

7. At this point, I suggest you use perhaps a quarter teaspoon of or a little more of salt for several cups of strips.

8. After that, you put the colander over a bowl and put a small plate on top to squeeze out the juice as it emerges.

9. Then you put some kind of weight on the plate such as a can of food, to speed things up.

10. In which you can leave it like this for an hour, or up to 24 hours (Note they get more solid over time, but most of the action happens in the first hour).

11. To make sure the brine is well distributed; I suggest you toss the strips with your fingers at some point.

12. Finally, you rinse the salt off and press the excess water out or you spread the "noodles" out on a cotton dishtowel (do not use terry cloth, or you may get lint).

13. At this point, the zucchini pasta is now ready.

14. It does not need to be cooked, but I suggest you gently warm it up.

15. Make sure you do not cook it too long, or it will stick together and/or become mushy.

Crust less Smoked Salmon, Leek, and Mushroom Quiche

Tips:

1. I suggest you use canned smoked salmon from Trader Joes, but any kind will work (though I have never tested it with lox-type salmon).

2. The Plain canned salmon is also great, too.

3. You can substitute the onions or shallots for the leeks (make sure you rinse carefully)

Ingredients:

1 ½ cups of milk, cream, unsweetened soy milk, or a combination of both (I prefer soy milk with a little cream)

1 large leek, with light green and white parts sliced (approximately one cup of slices)

4 oz. of raw mushrooms (preferable, wild or shitake are nice for this, but any will do)

1 teaspoon of dry mustard

4 eggs

6 ounces of salmon, or so smoked

1 small red pepper (chopped, about half a cup)

3/4 cup of shredded cheese (Note that almost any kind or combo is fine, but not too much strong-flavored cheese such as parmesan)

½ teaspoon of thyme

Paprika, salt, and pepper to taste

A pinch of cayenne pepper (or a bit of hot sauce)

Directions:

1. Meanwhile, you heat oven to a temperature of 375 F.

2. After that, you Sauté the leeks in a little olive oil, and when they begin to soften, add mushrooms.

3. After a minute or two, then you add the peppers.

4. After which you add a little salt, and cook for about 3-4 minutes.

5. Just before taking off heat, I suggest you add the thyme.

6. In the meanwhile, you crumble salmon in pie plate.

7. After which you cover with vegetables when done.

8. Then you sprinkle with the cheese.

9. In the meanwhile, I suggest you blend the eggs, milk (or other), mustard, cayenne or hot sauce, salt (approximately ½ teaspoon, but less if salmon is salty), and pepper.

10. You can also use an eggbeater or whisk, but a blender works fine.

11. At this point, you pour the egg mixture over the rest of the ingredients, and sprinkle with paprika.

12. Finally, you bake for 35-50 minutes.

13. Make sure you start checking after half an hour.

14. I suggest you cover with foil when it gets too brown but the middle is too liquid,

15. Remember that the center will still be a bit loose, when done.

16. At this point, you should take it out of the oven or the rest will overcook.

17. Note that in 5 minutes, the center will be done from the heat of the rest of it.

Nutritional value: per 6 servings

Amount per serving

Calories: 200

Carb: 2.5g

Protein: 18g

Dietary fiber: 2g

Zesty Grilled Shrimp

Tips:

1. Remember, that shrimp are so quick to cook, but the main danger is simply cooking them too long!

2. This is the easy and delicious method for turning out perfect grilled shrimp in just a short time.

Ingredients:

¼ cup of oil (preferable olive or any other of your choice)

¼ cup of soy sauce

2 cloves garlic (crushed)

Sugar substitute (equivalent to about 1 Tablespoon of sugar)

1 lb. of shrimp, shelled and deveined (for the size, I suggest you see note below)

3 Tablespoons of lemon or lime juice

2 Tablespoons of grated fresh ginger

1 teaspoon of dried thyme

¼ teaspoon of cayenne (or other dried hot pepper such as pepper flakes)

Directions:

The steps in choosing Shrimp:

1. Remember, that the larger the shrimp, the more expensive, and yet the easier to grill.

2. I prefer saving money by using medium-large shrimp labeled "20-25" (meaning that is how many you get in a pound).

3. After which, there are basically two procedure of grilling so they do not fall into the fire; the first is that you either put on skewers, or grill them on a rack or basket meant for vegetables.

4. I have also read of the idea of using a regular cake/cookie cooling rack for this, you just give it a trial.

How to Make the Marinade:

1. First, you mix the entire ingredients except for the shrimp together.

2. After which you taste.

3. At this point, you make adjustments and balance the flavors according to your tastes.

4. Note that the flavors will be a bit muted in the final dish; so I suggest you make it a little spicier than you want the shrimp to be.

5. If it seems too sour, I suggest you add a bit of sweetener.

6. Make sure the flavor is still bright, as the citrus will also be less sour in the by the time you marinate and cook with it.

7. Then you marinate the shrimp for about 15-20 minutes before grilling.

8. In addition, you put the shrimp on skewers if that is how you are doing it.

9. After which you heat the grill and oil the grill or rack.

10. Make sure the grill or rack is quite hot before putting the shrimp on.

11. Note that if the grill is hot they will cook in only 1-2 minutes on each side.

12. I prefer doing it on a vegetable rack. What I do is to lay them out, and almost as soon as I get them all laid out; I start turning the first ones over.

13. When they are just finished turning opaque all the way through, this is the point at which you know that they are ready.

Unstuffed Cabbage

Tips:

1. You can make this healthy recipe in either the oven or a slow cooker (crock-pot).

2. You can make use of a large, covered roasting pan, this is because the raw cabbage takes up so much space, but it shrinks a lot during cooking.

3. Remember that this version of recipe has the same flavors and ingredients of stuffed cabbage, but is much easier.

4. You can make this recipe as a low fat by using very lean ground meat.

5. If Eastern Europe does not have exciting enough flavors for you, I suggest you add some hot sauce to the tomatoes.)

Ingredients:

2 to 3 pounds ground meat (beef, turkey, combos, whatever), depending on the servings you want

2 Tablespoons of caraway seeds

2 teaspoons of garlic powder

6 Tablespoons of lemon juice (you can use vinegar, which is actually more traditional)

A salt, pepper to taste

2 head cabbage

½ cup of minced onion

2 teaspoon of ground coriander

2 can tomatoes (approximately 16 oz., diced is nice, but whole is fine)

Any sweetener of your choice

Directions:

1. First, you cut the cabbage into chunks, approximately 3 inches on a side (you do not have to be exact).

2. After which you separate into pieces, maybe 2 to 4 leaves thickness each.

3. Then you put about ½ in the bottom of the roasting pan or crock-pot.

4. At this point, you mix the meat, onion, and spices, including salt and pepper.

5. After which you form into meatballs, and nestle them amongst the cabbage leaves.

6. Then you put the rest of the leaves on top.

7. In addition, you put tomatoes and lemon juice or vinegar into blender, or into a pot and use a stick blender, or you use a food processor.

8. After which you pulse a few times.

9. If you want the tomatoes partially pureed, but still to have the chunks.

10. You can fully puree half the can, if you so wished.

11. You can carry this out in a pot on the stove and cook it down a bit, if you wish.

12. Then you add sweetener to the tomato mixture until you get a nice "sweet and sour" effect.

13. At this point, you add a bit of salt and pepper, and another tablespoon of caraway seeds, if you want.

14. After that, you pour the mixture over the cabbage.

15. Finally, you bake in oven at a temperature of 350 F for an hour.

16. I prefer covering it for the first 20 minutes to get the juices going, and then remove the cover.

17. If you using a crock pot, I suggest you cook for 6 to 8 hours on low or 2 to 3 on high.

Nutritional value: per serving

Amount per serving

Carb: 15g

Protein: 30g

Dietary fiber: 9g

Thousand Island Dressing

1. This recipe can be used on burgers, special sauce, with shrimp, and on a salad.

2. You should feel free to vary the balance to your own taste.

Ingredients:

½ cup of sour cream

6 tablespoons of relish (sugar-free).

½ cup of sugar-free ketchup

½ cup of mayonnaise

2 tablespoons of prepared mustard

DIRECTIONS:

1. First, you mix the ingredients together and adjust to your taste.

2. You might wish to add a little more ketchup or even some sweetener to it, depending on the exact ingredients.

Nutritional value:

Amount per serving size: 1 tablespoon

Calories: 35

Carbohydrate: 0.5g

Warm Spinach Salad with Hot Bacon Dressing

1. This spinach salad can easily be made into a meal, this can be achieved by adding chopped cooked chicken, turkey, or even fish or tofu.

2. If you want more vegetables, I suggest mushrooms and red pepper will be a good option.

Ingredients:

2 package of baby spinach (about 9-10 oz.) or that much washed spinach leaves

8 pieces of thick-cut bacon or 6 pieces thin cut (about 150 grams), chopped

½ cup minced onion

½ clove garlic

4 Tablespoons of cider vinegar (or the same amount as the bacon fat)

2 pinch of salt

4 pinches of pepper

4 teaspoons of worth sugar substitute

Directions:

1. First, you put the spinach (and other vegetables if you so wished) in a large bowl. (NOTE: The spinach will shrink down some in the hot dressing, but you need room to work).

2. After which you chop the bacon and fry until crisp.

3. Then remove with slotted spoon and drain on paper towels.

4. Furthermore, leave about 2 Tablespoons of the bacon fat in the pan, which is only if you like a lightly dressed salad.

5. Nevertheless, if you want more dressing, I suggest you leave more fat and then balance it with more vinegar and a bit more sweetener. (Have in mind that this dressing is a sweet and sour sort of thing.)

6. After which you cook the onion in the fat for about 2-3 minutes.

7. Then you add the garlic and cook for 15-30 seconds or until it is starting to be fragrant (note: Be careful not to brown the garlic or it will get bitter).

8. In addition, you add the vinegar, and scrape up the brown bits in the pan. (The vinegar will seem potent, but it mellows quickly with the heat and sweetener.)

9. After which you add salt, pepper, and sweetener.

10. Then you stir to dissolve.

11. Finally, you pour the dressing over the spinach.

12. After which you toss (tongs works perfectly well) until coated.

13. Then you transfer to individual plates or bowls and top with bacon bits and other toppings of your choice.

Nutritional value:

Amount per serving size: Each serving

Calories: 194

Carbohydrate: 3.5g

Dietary fiber: 2.5g

Protein: 9g

Watermelon Salad with Cucumber and Mint

TIPS:

1. This recipe is in such a way that you can easily adjust it to make many portions or a few.

2. Normally, it is ½ watermelons and ½ cucumbers with a sprinkling of mint and feta cheese.

3. Note that the saltiness of the cheese makes a surprisingly delicious contrast to the watermelon.

Ingredients:

3 cups of cucumber (chopped)

½ cup of crumbled feta cheese

3 cups of watermelon (chopped)

½ cup of minced fresh mint

Directions:

1. First, you mix the watermelon, cucumber, and most of the mint and cheese together.

2. After which you sprinkle remaining mint and cheese on top.

3. Then you garnish with whole mint leaves if you so wished.

Nutritional value:

Amount per serving size: Each of 8 serving

Calories: 33

Carbohydrate: 3.5g

Dietary fiber: 1g

Protein: 1g

Cream Cheese Frosting

Tips:

Remember that you can flavor this recipe in any way you want.

Note: This frosting goes very fine on a Low-Carb Spice Cake.

This recipe will occupy an 8" or 9" round or square cake in the pan.

This recipe is also good as a spread (do not add water).

Ingredients:

Liquid sucralose (equivalent to approximately 1 ¼ cup of sugar or to taste)

4 tablespoons of water

16 oz. package cream cheese

1 ¼ teaspoons of caramel flavoring

1 ¼ teaspoons of vanilla extract

Directions:

1. First, you use a mixer, combine the entire ingredients and beat until smooth.

2. For a spread, I suggest you do not add any water (Note: I use about ½ the sweetener of frosting when making a spread). Tips: use maple flavoring, or basically any type of your choice.

Nutritional value:

Amount per serving size: (Two tablespoons of spread, or one of eight servings of frosting)

Calories: 89

Carbohydrate: 0.5g

Protein: 2g

Banana Bread

Tips:

1. Preheat oven to a temperature of 350 degrees F.

2. After which you butter a loaf pan (I prefer the clay type)

Ingredients:

6 eggs

water

4 cups of almond meal

1 teaspoon of salt

4 medium bananas (very ripe)

4 tablespoons of oil

Zero-carb sugar (substitute to equal 1 cup of sugar)

2-tablespoon of baking powder

1 cup of chopped walnuts (it is optional)

Directions:

1. First, you roughly mash the bananas, and put in 2-cups measuring cup.

2. After which you add eggs and oil to cup.

3. If you are using liquid sweetener, I suggest you put that in as well.

4. When finish filling the cup to the 2-cup line with water. (If you only have a one-cup measuring cup, I suggest you just divide it up.)

5. Furthermore, you put almond meal, baking powder, and salt in bowl (if you using a powdered sweetener this when you add it) and stir to incorporate.

6. After which you add wet ingredients, and beat for about 2-3 minutes.

7. This is the point when you stir in walnuts if you are adding them.

8. Finally, you pour batter into loaf pan and smooth the top.

9. After which you bake for about 45-55 minutes, or until an inserted toothpick comes out clean.

10. Then you cool for about 10-15 minutes, and remove from pan.

11. Make sure you cool completely before slicing.

Nutritional value:

Amount per serving size: each of 12 servings

Calories: 147

Carbohydrate: 6g

Dietary fiber: 2g

Protein: 5g

Coconut Shrimp

Tips:

This sugar-free recipe you can use as an appetizer, party food, or main course.

Ingredients:

2/3 cup of coconut flour

½-teaspoon black pepper

4 eggs

Optional sugar substitute (equal to 2 tablespoons of sugar)

A cooking oil of your choice

2 pounds' large raw shrimp (peeled and deveined or you thaw if frozen)

½ teaspoon of cayenne pepper (or 2 teaspoons ancho pepper)

2 teaspoons of salt

4 tablespoons of water

1 cup of shredded coconut (unsweetened)

Directions:

1. First, you mix coconut flour with red, black peppers and salt. After which you whisk the eggs with a fork in a small dish.

2. Then you mix with the 4 tablespoons of water and add sweetener if you wish.

3. In addition, you put shredded coconut in a separate dish.

4. After which you put the oil in a large skillet to about 3/4-inch depth.

5. Then you heat to about 350 to 360 degrees (or until the end of a wooden spoon handle dipped into the oil collects bubbles around it).

6. Furthermore, you hold shrimp by the tail, roll in coconut flour, and shake to get most of it off (you only need a thin coating).

7. After which you dip in egg, again shaking off the excess.

8. Finally, you roll in coconut.

9. After which you fry the shrimp until it is golden on each side (approximately 2 minutes per side).

I prefer putting each in the pan as I prepare them, if you want to do it this way; I suggest you have to watch the ones in the pan closely (another way is to bread a few at once and then put them all in the pan at a goal. Do not overcrowd the pan, because it will reduce the temperature of the oil this makes them absorb more oil and will finally become heavy and greasy).

Note: Tongs are the effective tool for turning and removing the shrimp.

After which you remove from the pan to a paper towel or cooling rack.

When you want to serve, I suggest you serve with sweet and spicy dipping sauce, if you wish.

Nutritional value:

Amount per serving size: each of 3 servings

Calories: 434

Carbohydrate: 3g

Dietary fiber: 4g

Protein: 36g

CONCLUSION

These healthy recipes would help you Shred the Fat Instantly and keep the weight off for good. Get in shape this Season taking this Delectable recipe. If you follow religiously to the "IT STARTS WITH FOOD" THE WHOLE 30 By MELISSA HARTWIG and some of the recipes outlined in this book. You are going to be seeing results in 30 days, because it is proven to work.

Thank you and good luck!

www.ingramcontent.com/pod-product-compliance
Lightning Source LLC
Chambersburg PA
CBHW081727100526
44591CB00016B/2535